PLAYFUL
PATTERNS
COLORING BOOK

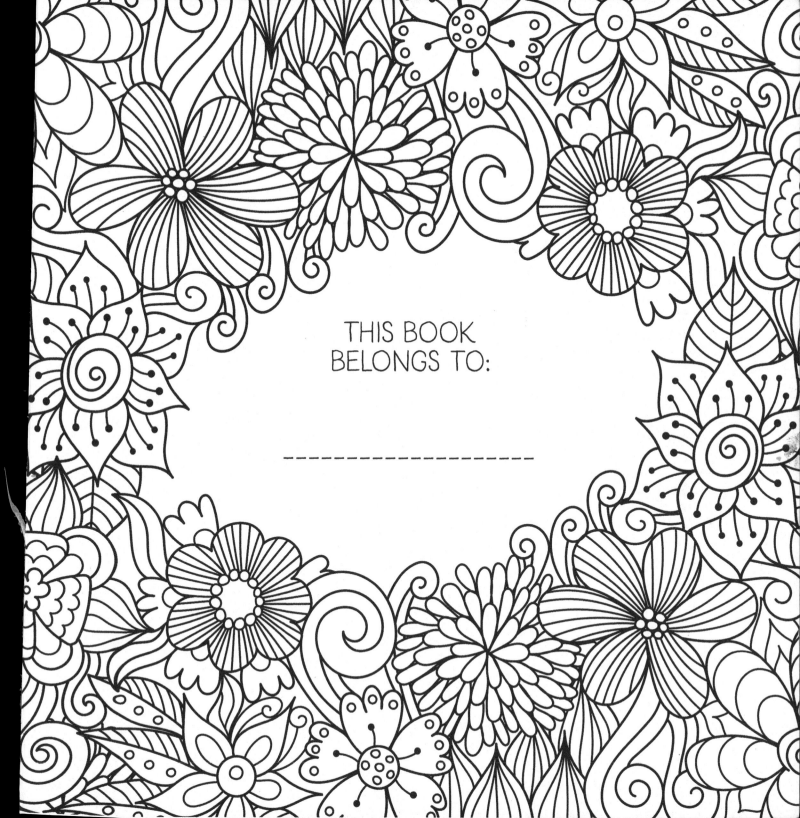

THIS BOOK
BELONGS TO:

_____

ALSO AVAILABLE - PRIMARY STORY JOURNALS

Primary Story Journal Composition Books

Grade Level K-2 Draw and Write Notebooks for Early Childhood to Kindergarten

Primary Story Journals feature writing lines at the bottom with a blank area for drawing at the top of every page. Your child can write stories, keep a daily journal, or even simply practice their handwriting.

7.5" x 9.25" (19.05 x 23.5 cm)
120 Pages each
Softcover Paperback

From Left to Right
Mermaid - 978-1718091467
Baby Unicorn - 978-1718152205
Spaceship Rocket - 978-1719862301
Cartoon Dinosaurs - 978-1719801942
Happy Dinosaurs - 978-1726724036

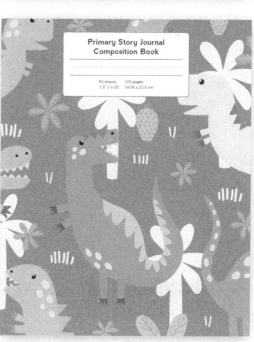

Made in the USA
Las Vegas, NV
06 May 2021

30 QUIRKY AND FUN DESIGNS!
SUITABLE FOR ALL AGES.

ISBN 9781719891905